# GABRIELLE INTEGRAL

## Gaetan Tremblay

Also from same author:

## GABRIELLE INTÉGRALE
(French Version)

## WORLDVIEW 5.0
An Answer to our Quest for Meaning
The Next Evolutionary Step for the West and
America

## VISION DU MONDE 5.0
Une Réponse à notre Quête de Sens
La prochaine Étape évolutionnaire pour
l'Occident et l'Amérique

Gaétan Tremblay
# Gabrielle Integral

INTACT Editions (Gaétan Tremblay) Longueuil, Québec, Canada.


ISBN  978-2-9814987-1-7
Bibliothèque et Archives nationales du Québec and Library and Archives Canada, 2014.

*To*

*Irene, Gaetan and Ian*

# Table of Contents

# A Bright Dream

The shadow of the night spreads slowly through the streets of my neighborhood. It illuminates many homes in its path. A candle on my bedside table greets this arrival of an imminent rest. Its flame stirred by a summer breeze creates animated silhouettes on the walls of my room.

Lying on my bed, I allow this improvised theater to distract my thoughts and dilute the reality of the day. Relaxed, my eyelids close like a heavy curtain. The mill of my thoughts slows to a stop in the hereafter of a day, which is then only a memory among so many others.

Here I am wandering again through the fog of my sleep and on the unknown stages of new dreams. What will the play of the intermixed memories of my unconscious and the projections of my free imagination bring to me?

A Daliesque landscape soon brightens my sleep. Near a collapsed heap of scratched tablets, an angelic silhouette illuminates this scene with its fairy light. My footsteps carry me to this bright being awakening in me some nebulous memories. I distinguish large eyes on the face of the stranger. Attracted by his look of vastness, I enter the aura of his encompassing light.

A penetrating voice like a sea breeze stirring the disillusioned sands of deserted beaches flies off his coppery lips:

– Do you recognize me?

– You seem familiar...

– My name is Gabriel.

Many paintings of instilled stories cross my mind to settle on the image of Gabriel, the messenger. I immediately continue:

– Are you Gabriel, the messenger?

Silence inspires me to go on.

– What do I owe the honor of meeting you?

He replied with a voice sounding released from a somewhat forced restraint.

– I am Gabriel announcing the return of the integrity of the world.

Gabriel suddenly turns to a shine so intense that it blinds me.

I suddenly wake up in the light of a new day. An untitled manuscript seems to crush my nightstand with its weight. I admit that my last manuscript is heavy, heavy of its subject, a worldview with a chain-and-ball around its feet. All things considered, though, my manuscript seems to me rather light, as light as a simple key.

Memories of my dream vivify the theater of my thoughts. A host of question and exclamation marks excite my heightened neurons. Has the Gabriel of my dream invited me to go beyond worldviews that reduce reality? Is he inciting me to journey to the country of found again fullness of the world? Is Gabriel my traveling companion?

My manuscript suddenly rises above its center of gravity, lightened from the weight of being untitled. I catch it in its flight. The name of Gabriel and more now appears on its embellished cover.

# The West' Binoculars

How to approach the West' worldview? Starting with the myths of the beginning? A big bang type fluctuation of a quantum field or potential? The universe? Earth? Life? Humanity? The purpose of existence? I almost feel like putting my tablet in its pocket and offering myself a tour of the world by bicycle and canoe.

Well, a worldview primarily concerns the world and a person or persons contemplating it. Human condition being what it is, we first see the world according to cultural parameters with which our eyes have adjusted through learning. We then affirm our personality and sometimes decide to enlighten our minds with new light.

With this in mind, an outdated refrain risks to distort any discussion of worldviews. It goes as follows: "Worldviews are culturally and individually subjective... One is just as good as the other... No one can claim to truth... There is no truth..."

I visualize a crowd jostling at the top of a twisted staircase of a tower of Babel. There prevails a general confusion. Individuals are trying to communicate with each other while systematically demolishing their mutual sayings. However, they all speak a common language, that of relativism and deconstruction.

Relativism suggests that all truth is subjective because a person or group with specific experience in a particular cultural context enunciates it.

The ideology of deconstruction, often under the influence of relativism, is busy dismantling any suggested thesis just for the sake of it. Ideological innovation and formulation of new societal projects therefore prove difficult. Especially if we add the influence of individualism always keeping its distance from any social project, being too busy looking at itself in a mirror.

It is true that no one will ever hold the complete truth. However, a fact remains. Truth is built over time, although it will never be exhaustive. Let's mention the end of Inquisitions, the Enlightenment and all the scientific, social and cultural progress accumulated since.

Other examples are the progressive recognition of universals such as respect for human dignity, freedom, social justice and solidarity. These universals will one day transcend all nations, cultures and their histories such as how mathematics transcend cultures and is not negotiable.

I cheerfully descend the spiral staircase of this tower of Babel, of circular cultures, and walk away as fast as I can. Strolling along a shoreline, something jutting out from the soil attracts my attention. It is binoculars with the word "West" engraved on its metal band. The lenses seem rather cloudy, probably due to the passage of time. I put it in my bag.

Once home, I disassemble the binoculars, curious to see the bright impressions that its lenses have absorbed through time.

Popping the lenses out a rush of images escape: half of a wheat field, a fragmented universe, scratched tablets, an angel's wing, some overheated neurons and a nothingness ill at ease to be... a non-being.

Once upon a time in the West there was a character of astounding lucidity. This man lived in a land divided up into many golden fragments of stars joining the blue of the sky and of the sea. A starry landscape embellished with busy pristine white villages. The name of this character was Plato, nicknamed as such because of his broad forehead.

Plato was a great thinker. He concluded that the world and the cosmos reveal a beautiful mutual harmony projected by a deity. Despite all the sensual beauty surrounding him, Plato argued that true knowledge couldn't have as its object the tangible world. This world being finite and changing, it is only fleeting illusions, according to this philosopher.

A sheep in the flesh for example is limited in time and space since it is condemned to die and disappear one day. The pure idea of sheep on the contrary is immutable and lasts infinitely; it will always be the same for all generations to come. Tangible and sentient beings are shadows of imperishable pure ideas of reason. These pure ideas are the true object of knowledge according to Plato.

Therefore, true reality lies in the minds of those who are aware of this phenomenon, the initiates. As initiates become familiar with the pure ideas of reason, the closer they get to the supreme pure idea, which is the deity. The deity is unattainable, but it is part of the world as evidenced by the universal and social harmony where everything and everyone occupy the place they should and deserve.

This line of thinking reduces the material and corporal world associated with illusion, finitude, change and time. Truth, infinity, immutability and timelessness are the domain of pure ideas and divinity. In short, this Platonic view fragments the world into material order, pure ideas of reason and the divine in a movement of visionary introversion.

The philosophies of Plato and his great followers that are Plotinus, Saint Augustine and Saint Thomas Aquinas defined the foundations of Christian doctrine. Christianity is not satisfied with merely fragmenting the world. It explicitly separates it. Reason and the divine tip over and end up in an esoteric realm preceding all existence. If our reason has difficulty to reconcile existence out of existence, it suffices to rely on faith.

Thus, on one hand there is a

patriarchal, divine, timeless, immutable and infinite realm located outside spatiotemporal existence. On the other hand, there is a fallen world because of Eve, patriarchal, temporal, changing and finite. In short, spirituality is separated and opposed to universal and earthly materiality.

Among this materiality, only enlightened or initiated human reason can claim to get close to divine spirituality and speak in its name.

Humanity or rather man thus has the luxury of statutorily separating himself of all that lives on earth, in the sea and the sky, dominating and taking ownership of it all, including woman declared responsible for this world now devoid of spirituality. Amen!

The sky rumbles, darkens and becomes threatening. I close my windows. I notice the West binocular' parts scattered on my table draw a silhouette resembling a question mark. I wonder.

May the West still favor such an approach to the world? Is spirituality really missing from the world?

Were the pyramids of absolute patriarchal earthly power legitimized by a triangle (Father-Son-Holy Spirit) of absolute patriarchal celestial power?

I collect the pieces of the binoculars, put them in a small sealed box and put everything on a shelf in my library.

The sky suddenly clears. I open my windows back to their full size, breathe a big breath of fresh air, put on my shoes and start a new world tour of my neighborhood.

# A Newly Found Lens

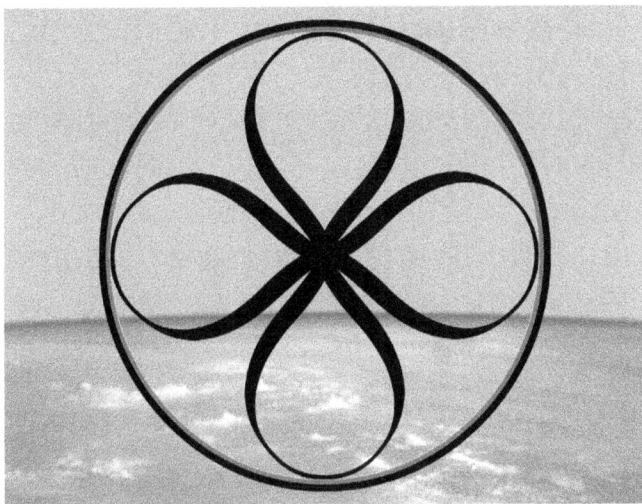

I decide to put aside the self-proclaimed stranglehold of monotheisms on spirituality to give free rein to my thoughts.

It seems that for most of us, spirituality refers to the non-tangible, non-material, non-finite and non-temporal. It is the feeling that something intangible, immaterial, infinite and timeless exists and lives in the world and us since we have such a feeling.

Then, I remember the strength of pantheistic and polytheistic movements throughout history. Some followers saw spirituality in everything while others visualized it through the symbolism of various gods and goddesses all part of this world. These spiritual movements obviously were not doing well with Christianity, which ejects spirituality out of this world and simplifies and reduces it to a single divine power. Political authorities, always interested in an increased concentration of power, obviously tended to ally themselves to Christianity in the repression of these spiritual movements.

A crow flies close to my head almost snatching a strand of my hair. I probably came too near its nest and offspring. I continue on my way.

So, spirituality is akin to what appears to exceed or transcend the finished side of things and time, the finite side of the three dimensions of space and the one of time. It is defined as infinity of these four dimensions, as infinity of the world. Is this infinity of the world only a shadow of an out of this world deity or rather a fact of this world, knowledge, but ignored by the scientific, cultural and spiritual discourse of our societies?

Einstein kindly answered this question. He made an indirect demonstration that the infinite is indeed a reality of our world. By stating that space and time cannot be separated. Time extends in space and space extends in time. Thus, they both exceed their boundaries through extending in one another. Space and time are continuous, hence the notion of space-time continuum. This continuum suggests a dimension of infinity proper to the very structure of space-time.

I stop at an intersection due to a red light. One more step and I would have crushed a large ant. The universe gives way to the world of elementary particles in my head.

Quantum physics concerns the behavior of the smallest observable amounts of energy. It is described as quantum because studied energy is manifested as quanta or clumps of particles. This energy also manifests itself as waves. That is why we often refer to a wave-particle duality.

A wave-particle not subject to scientific observation behaves as a wave and can be found here and there. Ubiquitous waves evolve into a global space. There is no difference between here and there. For a wave, space is not particularized, not delimited and not finite or yet space is total, one and infinite. A global space goes with a global time according to the continuity of space and time.

According to scientist Trinh Xuan Thuan, *"Here" is identical to "there." The universe is a vast system of particles all interacting on each other. Not content to have given a holistic nature to time, quantum mechanics also gives it to space... All the particles in the Universe... Are part of a same global reality.* [1]

The infinitely small and the infinitely large confirm each other and meet one another by way of their common dimension of infinitude. How can it be otherwise since they both describe a same reality, although from different point of view?

A comment from painter and poet William Blake comes to my mind to the effect that *if the doors of perception were cleansed, everything would prove to man, as it is, infinite.* [2]

Great mathematician Georg Cantor argued for his part that *the fear of infinity is a form of myopia that destroys the possibility of seeing the actual infinite...* [3]

Being ourselves stars and elementary particles products, being ourselves infinitely large and infinitely small, we all carry in the palm of our hands, our hearts and our neurons the dimension of infinity of reality.

I walk along a balcony. A young girl is counting multicolored blocks. By doing so, she is suggesting infinity. The little girl may count to ten or forever, there will always be a number that will succeed the last one that she mentioned.

Green light! I cross the road and continue around my neighborhood.

I wonder why science has not yet announced the infinite as a fifth dimension of the world, after the three dimensions of space and the one of time? Why the worldview of the West fails to include the presence of a dimension of infinity in reality? For what reason one of the basic foundations of any worldview - spirituality- is removed from this world?

It is true that science cherishes the study of the finite and its corollary predictability. Science has also long ago abandoned the issue of spirituality to religions to not get bogged down in controversies that would have certainly slowed its progress. It probably will avoid for yet another long time to draw a sign of equation between the infinite of the world and spirituality.

Such an equation would probably trigger a reactionary wave among the religious and scientific communities. More, what is to be said about the many political powers legitimizing their finite earthly kingdoms with an infinite celestial one.

One thing is for sure, infinite quantities are so frequent in mathematics that physicists tend to subtract them from their calculations to obtain approximate, but still practical models. Hermann

Wey even concludes that mathematics is effectively a science of the infinite. More over, mathematical language is that of scientific investigation and knowledge. In short, the very essence of knowledge evolves in the five dimensions that are the infinite, the three dimensions of space and the one of time.

In this perspective, the model of many cultures regarding that science and spirituality are two different and even opposing domains does not hold water. This model even came out with such ideas as the *war of worldviews* referring to a confrontation between spirituality and science.

It seems increasingly clear that such dualistic notions reveal cultures that persist with separating the world from its inherent spirituality. Cultures in conflict with the world and with themselves because of not pacified with the integrity of reality and their own integrity since they are of this world.

Spirituality or the infinite cannot exist out of existence or in nothingness or absolute vacuum, which is contradictory.

Infinity only makes sense by being, by being the infinity of something finite. Without finitude, infinity cannot even be imagined and defined. Infinity does not escape finitude more than the latter escapes the former. The two intertwine and are united in their state of being. Let's try to understand, a wee bit, the nature of this relationship in the context of experiences of spirituality and a new spirituality.

As much as the infinite leaves its mark through finitude, so finitude must make its mark on the infinite. Thus, all finite reality, concrete or abstract, our emotions, our thoughts and individual and collective action through time would resonate through the dimension of infinity of reality. The echo of this resonance would ring back through our earthly reality.

Such reciprocal influence of dimensions of finitude and infinitude suggests that humankind has contributed to this phenomenon throughout history. Logically, other intelligent species through the cosmos also contributed to this phenomenon through universal history. This interaction between the finite and infinite probably drives our intimate sense of being related to an infinitude or totality preceding our life and radiating through our present.

If we summarily define intelligence as the ability to link events, such a totality or infinity would be physically intelligent in that it connects all events, as in quantum physics and the space-time continuum.

This infinity would also be somehow consciously intelligent. Let's consider resonances on this dimension of infinitude of states of consciousness experienced through world history. This is saying a lot, if we consider the possibility, some scientists would say the likehood that the universe has always existed in one form or another. Note that the big bang theory still fits in such a scenario.

The dimension of infinitude connects all reality. It may thus appear superior to the finite dimension. This apparent superiority would explain a tendency to put it on a pedestal and to eventually deify it. It remains that infinitude is nothing if detached from the world or existence.

The architectural beauty of a church catches my eyes. I dwell upon it for a moment to contemplate.

…..

1. Trinh Xuan Thuan, Le Chaos et l'Harmonie, Gallimard, France, 1998, pages 351, 443.
2. Joseph Chilton Pearce, Spiritual Initiation and the Breakthrough of Consciousness, Park Street Press, 2003, p. 88.
3. Rudy Rucker, Infinity and the Mind, Bantam Books, New York, 1983, p. 46.

# Living Reality

The spirituality in us does not require emperor's clothing, gold and silver pedestals or temples. It is simple and as complex as the world it inhabits, which hosts it and gives it meaning.

We can certainly consider spirituality as a whole and revere it, but without deifying it as such; this would amount to denaturing it and reducing the finite world. We can deify it if we are so inclined, but only if we also deify all components of the world and the universe with it, including our own selves.

To give thanks to spirituality is to assume to our best its presence, being the infinity of the world, the unity and solidarity of all beings, harmony, peace, love and empathy as proclaimed by several great prophets. This experience doesn't mean an accomplished state or is not reserved to purists. It is mainly a constant personal reach to be in such an ideal state of being.

Some will say that people need a story with a beginning and an end, a tale and an idol with whom they can identify. The purpose of this is to reassure them with their existential genealogy and to meet their need for inspiration and guidance. Isn't this the ultimate success of many stories about the creation, the beginning and purpose of life?

But, why are some tales reducing of the world, depressing, making people feel guilty of being what they are? It should be noted in this regard that some of the messages of great prophets are not necessarily to be confused with the versions that some groups have made of them. In short, why not rather imagine a story without beginning or end, a constantly evolving narrative centered on an immediately accessible and inspiring character?

This story can indeed be without beginning or end. The reason being that the big bang is a transformation of something into something else. It cannot be the result of the transformation of a nothingness or vacuum into something real.

Scientists Stephen Hawking and Leonard Mlodinow argue that the universe was created from nothing, but while stating that the origin of the universe was a quantum event. [4]

An event cannot happen out of nothing or an absolute vacuum. It has to be an event of something, something therefore already in existence. Science probably calls this something *nothingness* because it is not yet manifested in terms of energy or wave-particles from the point of view of our space-time parameters.

That said, the before of the big bang has to be a quantum potential, whatever its exact nature, quantum potential therefore allowing possible fluctuations. That's why a new story of spiritual order can open itself to a past with an infinite horizon or have no beginning.

This story can also have no end. The universe will expand infinitely or will contract. In the latter case, perhaps there will be annihilation of space-time in which we evolve, but not annihilation of everything. There is rather transformation of our universal reality into something else. That something could be another big bang.

Such a transformative story without beginning or end broadens our horizons, makes us taller, energizes and inspires us. Starring our own person, radiating universal spirituality through our daily actions.

A personalized spirituality does not prevent grouping and rituals. As long as this spirituality is respected and its energy catalyzed on such occasions, and as long as it is not diluted or abdicated in the wake of the desire to control by some.

To each belong the terms of the implementation of his or her inherent spirituality. Gabriel the messenger is an ideal companion for an invitation to a renewed spirituality.

He indeed gathers and propagates all the qualities culturally associated with men or women. This unifying personality is projected in Gabriel's physical representation by religious art. He sometimes has more masculine features, sometimes more feminine.

In all continuity, Gabriel or Gabrielle is also the messenger of wholeness. He or she precedes the particularity of the three main monotheisms in that he or she intervenes in each of them. Gabriel(le) thus elevates him(her)self above their division to be the messenger for each and everyone, the messenger of a common spirituality. Gabriel(le) suggests a universal spirituality. "*Gabrielle*" announces a new spirituality, the union or infinity of the world, the newly found integrity of reality.

She thus reminds us of the dignity of all beings and of all women and men. Gabrielle also invokes the religious past of many while being able to transform the present of all and guide humanity towards a new horizon.

How to help us navigate through the often-turbulent waters of our responsibilities and daily activities?

Ouch! As I am strolling in an area of architectural heritage, a small piece of a roof tile hits me on the head. Is this the great debate of ethics and morality suddenly demanding my attention?

…..

4. Stephen Hawking and Leonard Mlodinow, *The Grand Design*, Bantam Books, New York, 2010, pp. 8, 131.

# Goodness

The question of ethics is often frightening in its complexity. What if this heaviness was a scarecrow?

All beings are equal in statute in that they all share the same action of existing, of being. They are all statutorily free to be what or who they are as they all exist as particular beings. All beings are solidary because they all share this equality and freedom.

This trilogy of freedom, equality and solidarity is inherent to human existence and to all beings. It constitutes a fundamental component of their integrity and dignity. Existence instantly proclaims this trilogy and is the very essence of a practical morality.

Our daily live imbued with universal spirituality naturally projects the infinity of the world and this existential morality via a respect for all life forms and humanism. Thus, our everyday life is the messenger of Gabrielle's message.

No! One doesn't crush spiders... And one doesn't burn the back of ants with a magnifying glass.

One also distances himself from the anthropic principle to the effect that mankind is the purpose of the existence of the universe. If the great whole is so favorable to human existence that it could only have been created for humanity, then there is a particular non-anthropic principle for everything else that exists in the universe. The anthropic principle flirts with anthropocentrism or narcissism of the human species.

The above trilogy arising from an existential morality also has the distinction of being inseparable. One undermines freedom if equality and solidarity are thwarted. Inequality implies status and rights not shared by all and consequently different freedoms for individuals. The lack of solidarity indicates statutory inequalities and differentiated freedoms.

Equality is mitigated by constraint and disunity. Constraint or lack of freedom suggests relationships of superiority and inferiority and a lack of solidarity evokes statutory inequality.

Solidarity is distorted by inequality and coercion. Inequality categorizes by status, rights and freedoms not applicable to one and all. Constraint divides into oppressors and oppressed.

However, many Western societies favor freedom while neglecting equality and solidarity. The results are equality turning into a growing social and legal injustice; a lack of solidarity shown by individualism, several union selfishness, corporatism and interested politic; and finally liberties being increasingly restricted in the name of preserving freedom.

A morality emerges from existence or the world itself. This morality is to first respect the inseparable trilogy mentioned. The day the interrelatedness of these three universals will not be negotiable is obviously not for tomorrow. How can we help ourselves in the meantime to apply such a morality?

By reminding us of a simple guidance from philosopher Immanuel Kant, a guide requiring only a little imagination. He suggests that any norm of conduct that we adopt be evaluated by its potential consequences if it was to be adopted as a universal law.

Kant suggests to simply taking actions towards others, as we would like others to take towards us. Or still not to act against others in a way that we would not like others to act against us.

The mere evocation of this universal imperative quickly directs our thoughts, sayings and actions in the right direction.

Is this a return to the Christian imperative? No, because the Christian imperative is framed and managed by a monotheist religious doctrine with a particular conception of spirituality. Kant's imperative comes from individual freedom and its corollary responsibility. It is more consistent with spirituality inherent in the world and people.

It is true that our conscience being free, it can be creative in terms of goodness and less good. The practice of an existential ethic and universal imperative brings goodness and humanism. On the contrary, we show irresponsibility towards others and nature if we don't manage our freedom with this ethic and imperative.

Let's reflect for a moment on values currently carried by many of our cultures. Our primary instinct dictates personal survival and genetic reproduction. This instinct kicks off in each one of us a dynamic of aggression or escape on one hand and of domination for the power of procreation on the other hand. Thus, individualism, fear, violence, competition, power and sexuality make a primary mixture infallibly asking for the attention of our consciences.

It is not surprising that this particular mix of values is the main trademark of our cultures. Don't we, indeed, meet here with the darling cultural models of the worldview of the West? These models being political and religious manipulation of fear, glorification and marketing of violence, individualism, competition, power and all that is sexual.

Our challenge is to assume, control and sublimate our primary instinct and its values. Otherwise, this instinct is abandoned to the normative winds of ubiquitous marketing programs. It is then grabbed for a purpose other than individual and collective conservation, for irresponsible corporate profit.

A laissez-faire attitude towards our manipulated primary instinct is from now on self-destructive as evidenced by the state and direction of the world.

Individual and collective initiative is certainly more constructive than fear. Empathy is more rewarding than violence. Solidarity is more productive for everyone than individualism. Well-understood competition also calls for collaboration, contribution and synergy. Real power is about promoting win-win solutions rather than crushing others. Sensuality and sexuality can be fully experienced for themselves.

Passing an electronics store, I notice a giant TV screen broadcasting an advertisement. It shows what we are talking about...

The practice of an existential ethic and universal imperative in the light of an embodied spirituality has probably another benefit. The satisfaction of having done well, thus of having created positive imprints on the dimension of infinity and its echo in the world, the benefit of having prepared oneself for a peaceful death.

That said, where does our respect for others or respect for our own self by others begin? It begins with respect for our mother and father, the Earth, and our great family that is the biosphere.

# Our Large Family

I only have to cross a street to get to a favorite park where I can rest. I love its curved pond and illuminated fountain. At night it reminds me of the shape of my bedside lamp. I spot an inviting patch of sunny green with a bench.

The land is our mother and our father. The pampered babies and the neglected wise persons, the lovers and the lonely are our brothers and sisters. The birds humming the song of a unique and fragile biosphere are our friends. The majestic trees joining the depths of the earth and sky are a reminder of our infinite greatness.

All beings in the biosphere that arrive along with us to the finish line that is the current state of the evolution of life on Earth are our family. Component ecosystems of the biosphere being interdependent, we all indeed arrived here and now as members of a single team. A wind of spirituality or infinity or solidarity is blowing through the biosphere and inflating the wings of Gabrielle living in each one of us.

The overall behavior of the human species towards the planet, flora and fauna doesn't reflect, as it should the integrity of the world. Let's imagine a sporting contest (evolution), a winning team (current biodiversity) and one member (humanity) of this team proclaiming himself to be the only winner, not only ignoring the contribution of its team mates, but also undertaking to annihilate them. Such is the actual attitude of humanity towards the biosphere.

Climate changes caused by human activity are an example of a disrespectful attitude towards our vital environment. This disrespect is mirrored to us by the exponential multiplication of the impacts of these changes on the well being of our species. One of these major impacts is the increasing acidity of oceans resulting in a devastation of vital food chains.

This reminds me something of the kind... *To not act against others in a way that we would not like others to act against us...* To respect the biosphere is to respect future generations and us.

# Youths and Models

What an appropriate comment, the crying of a newborn baby! He is removed from his mother's womb, from his intimate world so that he can be born into another world. His complete union with his mom is broken, a situation creating a potential for serious anxiety and risks giving the baby a bad first impression of the world.

By immediately giving the baby a sense of security, we contribute to his adaptation to his new environment and lay the foundation for his socialization.

Days, months and early years following the birth of the child are of paramount importance. Parental absence may arouse his anxiety. The presence of at least one parent provides attachment and emotional continuity, adding to the child's sense of personal security and socialization.

Especially since the primary relationship of the child with the world must be experienced in the availability and particular attention of one or several adults. This allows adults to react adequately to the child who sporadically uses a natural aggressiveness to probe his surrounding world and construct his identity, which has for effect to guide and sublimate this tendency.

Is it a good idea to have a baby or very young child in a more or less attentive daycare where he will always be one among many others?

If the separation of the baby from his parents is normalized shortly after birth, will we be surprised by some of the potential issues that may arise later? … *I'm being separated from my parents, I might separate myself from my parents, my family, my schoolmates, my school, others, society...*

What about more and more severe and widespread depression in children and the attention deficit disorder with hyperactivity (ADHD) affecting an increasing number of children? The whole mainly approached from a medical point of view and treated (!) with millions of prescription drugs for very young children, youth and adolescents. Some picture...

Children, youth and adolescents acquire their values by observing behaviors around them. Parents, teachers, leaders and adults must practice what they preach. Otherwise, it's fracturing of the young mind, conceptually speaking. Faced with questionable parental attitudes or cultural patterns, our Emma and William may suffer from identity vertigo and exhibit behavioral problems. Examples of such models come to mind.

The tendency of many televised media is to reduce man in couple relationships thereby promoting the insight of women. Why such an historical turnabout? It is likely due to the growing purchasing power of women and the paramount importance of their decisions with respect to family expenses. Flatter to profit!

This tendency suggests that it is appropriate to reduce men, as it was previously so to reduce women? Why do our cultures profit from the reduction of one by the other? Doesn't such promotion of inequality divide and seed confusion among the minds of young people looking for meaningful norms, for a harmonious identity?

What about violent images broadcast by television and peddled by video games? They influence the brain toward violence, fuel the propensity for violence, raise our threshold of tolerance for violence and suggest a hostile world. Responsibility of these phenomena falls in the hands of adults and policy makers who don't follow up on this scientific knowledge.

The problem of youth violence is the one of an adult world enmeshed in outdated values of a not assumed primary instinct.

Another example of questionable cultural models is the glorification of competition. It certainly has its place in the world, but it becomes problematic when it becomes the operating system of cultures.

We all have witnessed sports competitions between youths,

sponsored by adults and leading to displays of questionable behavior. The pleasure of playing and learning for young people is replaced with the anxiety of the obligation to win or not to lose. Adults yell obscenities at children, bicker among themselves and publicly promote verbal and physical abuse.

There is also a cultural assumption that team sport gives young people a sense of cooperation, emphasizes socialization and defuses incivility and violence? Yet studies show a widespread culture of violence among the coaches and players of many sports. So that the practice of team sports, although it can serve positive purposes within the team, can degenerate into a strategic promotion of violence to achieve victory over another team. In this sense, ...*the activity of sport rather entails an increased level of aggressiveness among players and a decrease of moral conscience.* [5]

Why promote research if the knowledge gained is not acted upon? Are we determined to cling to some futile cultural models? Are we somewhat going in circles as society? Do we assume the integrity of the world through the preferred values and models of our cultures? Are we projecting Gabrielle' lights? Are we going forward?

Let's imagine the impact on our society if youths would evolve under the influence of cultural models of freedom, equality, solidarity, collaboration, cooperation, contribution and synergy. What kind of society would then be created? Probably a much different one than the one modeled by a certain dome of shame.

.....

5. Olivier Rascle, Dominique Bodin, *Le Sport est-il Source de Violence?* L'essentiel Cerveau et Psycho, Novembre 2011 -Janvier 2012, p. 55.

# A Dome and Its Vortex

Back at home; I decide to fully enjoy this beautiful day. I am now riding my bike. The Capitol building is in sight.

Images and words intertwine in my head to form a series of collages. Good and bad... Heroes and antiheroes... Chicago, Woodstock, San Francisco... Liberation of women and men... Freedom, justice, solidarity... Love and peace... Imagination... A whiff of hope gone wrong suddenly disturbs me. The Capitol is close by.

This dome is housing a strange stage, starring a cacophony of bipartisanship, lack of compromise and polarization.

Like a tower of Babel, a theater of the absurd, of power misunderstood, without overview, a whirlwind of self-destruction. Why is the Capitol sagging as a failed cake?

The social contract of the nation was yet imbued with humanism. Of course, the foundation of the republic was part of the colonial movement of European powers. The Promised Land was also released by cutting the ground from under the Aboriginal people and relegating the survivors on reservations scattered over a desolate territory. All catalyzed by the work of millions of slaves spread south and north.

However, the founding of the republic was marked by certain humanism for many. The poverty-stricken people coming from Europe were now taking advantage of the equal rights (equality) for each and everyone (solidarity) to free (freedom) acquisition of properties.

People had to work very hard to provide the means to acquire and retain property of any kind. When working by the sweat of his brow six days a week, one can't take care of public affairs and good government. People sovereignty ultimately falls in the hands of representatives via a political system of representation. In the hands of wealthy people, free to attend to public affairs.

Such a representative system creates an uprooted, elastic and disoriented sovereignty. Peoples are sovereign. Governance belongs to them and they govern representatives. Representatives cannot therefore claim to govern their rulers or the peoples. Yet they govern in practice. Thus, representatives monopolize people's sovereignty without actually doing it. They take responsibility for the conduct of affairs of the state, but without actually taking it since they only represent the peoples. Sovereignty is fragmented and adrift.

So that the common good, defined by representatives more or less sovereign and responsible, becomes easy prey for manipulators and profiteers that define it to their advantage.

Especially since poor immigrants seek satisfaction of their never satisfied desires, rather than their needs for a reasonable comfort. So they maintain a representative system even after the formation of a middle class. All orchestrated in all the living rooms of society by the promoters of marriage of consumption and representative system, by the profiteers of the status quo.

I pedal at full speed. The Capitol becomes gradually clouded in the back mirror of my bicycle.

Fortunately I can vote every day on as many topics as I want through the Internet. Why not a direct democracy for my country? Why this bipartisan, paralyzing, suffocating and self-destructive polarization?

After all, democracy is not a system per se, but an ideal and ideology whose practical experience is subject to the creativity of nations and the passage of time. Democracy and representative democracy are not synonymous. The second is only a particular experience of the first.

May as well ask the profiteers of the status quo to do hara-kiri ... Too bad ... Although a gathering of people across or beyond the major parties is always possible, if unlikely. Who will hold the torch for the common good of the United States, for an American Renaissance and who will follow Gabrielle?

I will still not let a bitter feeling about the Capitol spoils such a beautiful summer day. Sparkling white doves are fluttering in the sky. They seem to write a message on the blue sky, one of looking higher and deeper, of seeing the light of infinity or spirituality of the world, a message of living fully.

I roll, roll and roll on my white and blue bicycle to finally stop at a market. A tiny flower rears the tip of its nose between a few blades of grass on the counter of a florist. Where do you come from little flower? How did you get here? It just smiles at me in the middle of its beautiful yellow crown, yellowed by its evolution through time.

# Time Forward

Time can be divided in hours, minutes and seconds to which we can be accountable to the point of enslaving us. However, it still retains its fluidity thanks to the infinity passing through it. This infinity gives a direction to time, a past-present-future order and a forward momentum. Such a time forward allows universal history, life, evolution and diversification of nature.

How can infinity be behind this time forward, behind this irreversibility, this impossibility of going back in time? Then I imagine a machine to travel through time and I get in. Before putting it in motion, I must choose a present and a past time in order to program my machine to travel between these two specific moments.

Let's see. The past moment chosen must be defined. So I have to give an account of the precise nature of a past moment to pretend to get to it. This means that I have to fully grasp or understand the very nature of this moment or past event, being the state of the universe at that time. The problem is that no one can make such claim.

Understanding of an event and all its possible relations with its environment and comprehending of all possible relationships of this set with its environment and so on, understanding the universal system at a specific time proves an infinite project.

Such a project is of course practically impossible, but also for the simple and ultimate reason that the infinite is a specific part of the nature of any event and that the infinite cannot be encapsulated. Famous mathematician Georg Cantor established mathematical infinities and orders of magnitude between them, but stressed that the infinite in itself cannot be captured by its very nature.

A similar problem applies to the knowledge of the moment from which we would start our journey to the specific past time as well as to each intermediate time between the event of departure and arrival. Our trip to the past is all the more impossible considering that the number of these intermediate times is ultimately infinite.

Even if we could go beyond the impossible, our arrival at a specific past would alter its nature or its original integrity, which would therefore not be a return to this past.

Infinity jammed the pistons and circuits of my machine to travel through time. This spirit or spirituality of the world prevents the winding of time on itself and thus the collapse of space because one doesn't stand without the other.

It is useless to try to start my machine to travel through time. Gabrielle smiles at me on the screen of its control console.

A glance at my watch tells me that an infinite time has passed. I'm going home. See you little flower!

# A Beautiful Story

I approach my house. A pink sun bathes my neighborhood and reminds me to make a call. I light my full reserve of candles. The night will be beautiful.

My apple red velvet sofa is attracting me like a magnet. Ding! Dong! Someone is at my door. I get up hastily, tumble down a seemingly eternal long staircase, pick up a bouquet of flowers I had ready for this moment and I answer the door.  As hoped...

  – Gabrielle!

  – Good evening! Flowers... My favorite... Thank you!

We walk back up to the living room while Gabrielle plunges her angelic face into her bouquet of roses. Her blue-green eyes are then drawn to my manuscript on a coffee table. Gabrielle, her black sundress contrasting beautifully with her porcelain skin, approaches the table.

She looks at the cover of my manuscript, opens it, goes through the contents, closes it, turns to me and gratifies me a knowing smile...

www.ingramcontent.com/pod-product-compliance
Lightning Source LLC
Chambersburg PA
CBHW071843020426
42331CB00007B/1831